TRUMPETER SWAN

GIANTS AMONG US

Jason Cooper

Rourke Book Co., Inc.
Vero Beach, Florida 32964

Edited by Pamela J.P. Schroeder

PHOTO CREDITS
All photos © Lynn M. Stone

Library of Congress Cataloging-in-Publication Data
Cooper, Jason, 1942-
    Trumpeter swan / by Jason Cooper.
        p. cm. — (Giants among us)
    Includes index.
    Summary: Describes the physical characteristics, habitat, and
behavior of the heaviest native bird in North America.
    ISBN 1-55916-187-6
    1. Trumpeter swan—Juvenile literature. [1. Trumpeter swan.
2. Swans.] I. Title. II. Series: Cooper, Jason, 1942-
Giants among us.
QL696.A52C665   1997
598.4'184—dc21   96-52096
                                              CIP
                                              AC

Printed in the USA

TABLE OF CONTENTS

THE TRUMPETER SWAN

With its long neck and great wings, the trumpeter swan is a giant among birds. The trumpeter weighs more than any of North America's native birds.

Trumpeters are not only big, they're loud! They have a giant's voice box. Their calls sound like a horn blowing *ko-hoo, ko-hoo.*

Like their duck and goose cousins, trumpeters have waterproof feathers and wide, webbed feet. The webbed feet make good paddles for swimming.

The trumpeter swan is the heaviest of North America's native flying birds.

WHITE WIDE BODIES

A big, male trumpeter can weigh 30 pounds (13 kilograms). It can be more than 5 feet (1.5 meters) from its black bill to the tip of its tail. The trumpeter's wings are more than 7 feet (2 m) from tip to tip.

The only flying bird heavier than a swan is the **bustard** (BUS tard) of Europe.

Mute swans can weigh as much as trumpeters. Mute swans are not native to North America. They came from Europe.

A 25-pound adult trumpeter makes its two-day-old cygnet look tiny.

WHERE TRUMPETER SWANS LIVE

Trumpeter swans live in Alaska, western Canada, and the central Rocky Mountains. Small flocks, or groups, live in Minnesota, Iowa, Michigan, Ohio, Oregon, Wisconsin, Nebraska, Kansas, South Dakota, and Ontario.

Trumpeters live in many kinds of wet **habitats** (HAB uh tats), or homes. They like marshes, slow-moving rivers, and shallow lakes. Swans can dip their necks in shallow water to reach underwater plants.

Trumpeter swans like cattail marshes, like this one in Minnesota.

CYGNETS, THE BABY SWANS

A mother swan and her mate build a nest of marsh plants. Often they build on top of a muskrat's dome-shaped house.

The female swan usually lays five eggs. Her babies, called cygnets, begin to feed themselves almost as soon as they hatch.

First, cygnets eat insects and other little animals. Later they live largely on a diet of plants.

Young trumpeters are gray. They begin to fly three or four months after they hatch.

A trumpeter with its cygnet stands at their nest atop a muskrat's lodge.

A trumpeter paddles with its four gray cygnets in a marshy pond.

SWAN FOOD

Adult trumpeters usually eat **aquatic** (uh KWA tihk), or water-loving, plants. "Duck potato," an aquatic plant with large, white flowers, is a favorite food.

Trumpeters feed by using their strong, flat bills to break off pieces of plants. They find underwater roots by sweeping mud away with their feet.

Adult swans have no natural enemies. They use their snakelike necks, bills, and wings to defend their young. Cygnets are sometimes grabbed by **predators** (PRED a torz) such as snapping turtles, minks, and coyotes.

Looking like a white pillow, a "headless" trumpeter feeds on aquatic plants.

TRUMPETER SWAN HABITS

Trumpeters spend most of their time on or near water. They paddle ashore to nap and **preen** (PREEN). Birds preen by using their bills to clean and oil feathers. The swans' body oil waterproofs feathers.

Some trumpeter flocks migrate. **Migrations** (my GRAY shunz) are long journeys. Trumpeters may migrate several hundred miles from nesting areas to winter homes. Cold is not a problem for trumpeters, but they need to be where their food is not under ice.

Some flocks of trumpeters migrate from nesting grounds to ice-free winter homes.

TRUMPETER SWAN COUSINS

The trumpeter swan's closest cousin in North America is the tundra swan. Tundra swans are slightly smaller than trumpeters. A tundra swan usually has a small yellow patch at the base of its upper bill.

Tundra swans nest in northern Alaska and Arctic Canada. They migrate south from their nesting grounds in huge flocks each autumn. They spend the winter along the Atlantic and Pacific coasts of the United States.

In Europe, the whooper swan is almost a twin of North America's trumpeter.

All tundra swans nest in the Arctic and migrate south in winter.

PEOPLE AND TRUMPETER SWANS

Trumpeter swans used to live across much of what is now the northern United States. Settlers killed thousands of trumpeters for meat and feathers. The big wing feathers made excellent writing pens. Women wore clothes and hats decorated with swan feathers.

The big, white swans were easy targets. By the 1930s, the great, graceful trumpeter had nearly disappeared, except in Alaska.

Guarding its mate and nest, a male trumpeter challenges a wildlife scientist at the Kellogg Biological Station in Michigan.

SAVING THE TRUMPETER

Trumpeter swans have come back with the help of people. By 1968 scientists counted 3,722 trumpeters in North America. They counted 19,756 trumpeters in 1995!

Trumpeters are protected from hunters. Many of their nesting areas are protected, too.

Trumpeters are also helped by **captive breeding** (KAP tihv BREE ding). Captive birds nest and produce cygnets. The cygnets born in captivity are released into the wild. Scientists send them to states where trumpeter swans have not nested for more than 100 years.

Glossary

aquatic (uh KWA tihk) — of the water; living on or in the water

bustard (BUS tard) — a large, slow-flying bird with a heavy body and long legs; a cousin of cranes

captive breeding (KAP tihv BREE ding) — the raising of rare wild animals in zoos, often for release back into the wild

habitat (HAB uh tat) — the special kind of place where an animal lives, such as a *northern* marsh

migration (my GRAY shun) — travel to a distant place at the same time each year

predator (PRED a tor) — an animal that hunts other animals for food

preen (PREEN) — to carefully clean and oil feathers

INDEX